GARAGE
BANDS™

MANAGING YOUR BAND

DANIEL E. HARMON

rosen publishing's
rosen
central®

NEW YORK

Published in 2012 by The Rosen Publishing Group, Inc.
29 East 21st Street, New York, NY 10010

Library of Congress Cataloging-in-Publication Data

Harmon, Daniel E.
Managing your band/Daniel E. Harmon.—1st ed.
    p. cm.—(Garage bands)
Includes bibliographical references and index.
ISBN 978-1-4488-5659-6 (library binding)—
ISBN 978-1-4488-5663-3 (pbk.)—
ISBN 978-1-4488-5667-1 (6-pack)
1. Rock groups—Vocational guidance—Juvenile literature. I. Title.
ML3795.H324 2012
781.64068—dc22

                                                        2011017458

Manufactured in the United States of America

CPSIA Compliance Information: Batch #W12YA: For further information, contact Rosen Publishing, New York, New York, at 1-800-237-9932.

CONTENTS

INTRODUCTION ... 4

CHAPTER ONE
THE BAND MANAGER OR MANAGEMENT TEAM ... 7

CHAPTER TWO
ROAD WORK ... 16

CHAPTER THREE
MINDING THE MONEY ... 25

CHAPTER FOUR
LEGAL MATTERS ... 35

CHAPTER FIVE
SECURITY AND INSURANCE ... 45

GLOSSARY ... 54
FOR MORE INFORMATION ... 56
FOR FURTHER READING ... 58
BIBLIOGRAPHY ... 60
INDEX ... 62

INTRODUCTION

A garage band doesn't need to be managed—as long as it remains in the garage. When it goes public, though, management decisions have to be made. Someone has to see to unforeseen details and problems. Very quickly, the band's manager may become as important for success as any of the musicians.

When they first begin to jam and develop a unique style and sound, few young garage band members are thinking of music as a business. They just want to get together, have fun, and find out how good they are as individuals and as a group. Little do they realize what will be involved if they pursue professional music careers.

The time for garage players to take band management seriously is when they agree they have the makings of a play-for-profit performing act. Entertainers and athletes legally turn pro (or semipro) when they begin performing for money. By the time they play their first gig and

TO THE AUDIENCE, A PERFORMANCE MAY APPEAR TO BE ALL FUN AND MUSIC. BEHIND THE SCENES, HOWEVER, PLAYERS AND THEIR HELPERS MUST TAKE CARE OF COUNTLESS NONMUSICAL DETAILS.

receive their first paycheck, the band should have at least a basic system of management in place. How will the nonmusical aspects of their work be carried out? Who will handle the sound and stage equipment? Who will provide transportation? Who will have the authority to commit the band to future bookings? Who will handle the money, and how will it be divided?

In his book *Start Your Own Band*, author and professional musician Marty Jourard raises a question that strikes a chord with most garage musicians: "Why can't we just play music for the people, man?" He answers his own question: "Because it is, after all, called the music business."

You can play your music in a garage or basement as long as you want without managing anything. You're completely independent. But if you expect to earn a living at it—which, after all, is the dream of most garage musicians—you'll have to proceed in a businesslike way. And in any business, you need management.

Good music managers are not easy to come by. A band should take great care when choosing its manager or management team. Besides understanding how the music scene works, the manager has to be thoroughly familiar with the band's distinctive sound. The manager should understand the musicians' personalities, relationships, and joint goals. The band needs a manager who will be dedicated, long term, to its success.

For their part, the best band managers are picky in taking on a little-known band. It's a risky challenge. They might spend dozens of hours working with a group that breaks apart after a few performances—a horrible investment. They may find themselves representing a band whose players are embroiled in all sorts of distracting entanglements that have nothing to do with music. A smart manager will investigate carefully before becoming attached to a young garage band.

Members of a budding garage band may decide to manage themselves, at least for awhile. Sooner or later, if they become paid performers, they'll realize certain tasks should be turned over to other people—a manager and/or support team.

THE BAND MANAGER OR MANAGEMENT TEAM

In *All You Need to Know About the Music Business*, author Donald Passman discusses the professional band's ideal "team"—nonmusicians the band needs for support. A good team, Passman suggests, includes a personal manager, business manager, roadie(s), lawyer, and agent or agency.

Garage bands just starting out can't afford to hire so large a staff. They're doing well to employ just one "manager." Most garage bands expect this person to be their business and personal manager as well as their equipment-toting roadie. This basic manager obviously isn't a lawyer but should be able to know when they need a lawyer and find them a good one. Managers of many bands are also expected to serve as promoter, publicist, and booking agent.

What Does a Band Manager Do?

The role varies among bands. Usually, management duties for a fledgling garage band include the following.

Handling or Overseeing Physical Chores

Musicians naturally want to devote their time and energy to making music. Having a manager or small crew to attend to the nonmusical tasks involved in a performance gives them greater freedom to focus on their skills and stage presentation.

The main part of this role is the physical work required before and after a performance. Some managers literally move, set up, and take down stage equipment. Others employ one or more roadies (or find volunteer roadies, if the band can't afford to pay) to perform the labor.

Taking Care of Business

The manager makes the band's business decisions or plays a major advisory role. The business of music includes processing the agreements and paperwork entailed in performance commitments and recording. It involves equipment shopping and purchasing. Arranging publicity—selecting and hiring a photographer and publicist, buying

THE PERFORMERS RECEIVE THE PUBLICITY. BUT EVERY SUCCESSFUL BAND HAS AN EFFECTIVE MANAGER OR MANAGEMENT TEAM TO TAKE CARE OF THE BUSINESS SIDE OF ITS MUSIC.

and distributing promotional materials, and so on—is a business function.

Any area of the band's work that relates to money and property, from writing checks to arranging transportation to maintaining and replacing sound gear, calls for good business

DOES A BAND NEED A MANAGER?

Sheila E. Anderson, author of *How to Grow as a Musician*, answers: "Some do and some don't."

Veteran musicians point out that some beginning bands simply aren't ready for a manager. At their local level of performance, they can handle everything themselves, from promotion to booking to stage preparation. For those bands, in fact, a manager might be more of a complication than a benefit. Some young bands are all too eager to get down to business; they choose managers hastily and pay dearly for it. Good or bad, a manager is an extra person to take a share of the pay.

Although some managers can help musicians find new opportunities, others—especially novices—annoy the insiders. Anderson, a noted host and producer of TV and radio jazz programs, observes, "As a presenter, I deal with my share of managers, and they can tip the scales of whether I will hire an artist that I don't know well."

Before selecting a manager, band members should carefully discuss and agree on exactly what they want the individual to do for them.

sense. The manager needs to be a shrewd businessperson devoted to securing the band's best interests.

Marty Jourard, in his book *Start Your Own Band*, writes, "Artists are by definition creators; managers should do all they can to keep them away from direct contact with the business side of life, while at the same time keeping them well informed."

Promoting the Band

For some garage bands, the manager serves as booking agent and/or publicist. For others, that responsibility goes to a different member of the team—or is shared by everyone. In either situation, the manager usually is involved to some extent in efforts to make the band famous.

For local and regional acts, promotion requires grassroots work: compiling mailing lists of media contacts and fans, scrounging for coverage in a weekly newspaper, getting a demo recording played on the local radio station, and talking up the band through Facebook, Twitter, and other popular social media platforms.

LOCAL DISC JOCKEYS CAN GIVE NEW BANDS EARLY PUBLICITY AND AIR-PLAY. THE MANAGER IS THE BAND'S GO-BETWEEN WITH DJS, ENTERTAINMENT REPORTERS, AND OTHER MEMBERS OF THE MEDIA.

At a higher level, leading band managers are known and respected by recording companies' A&R representatives. These managers are in a position to bring the band to the attention of industry insiders, which could lead to a recording contract.

Communicating and Negotiating

The manager is the band's main go-between in relations with nightclub owners and other employers, recording companies, music industry agents, producers, radio personalities, music publishers, lawyers, the press, and the public.

Overseeing Internal Affairs

To succeed, the players all must be on the same page. It's the manager's responsibility to make sure they remain jointly focused as they progress and undergo changes.

Frequently, success brings unforeseen complications. More bookings for the band mean more scheduling conflicts. With heightened popularity, egos may clash. Invariably, bands undergo changes—changes in music, personnel, equipment, and individual goals.

Members fight (or at least argue) from time to time. Everyone has a unique personality and set of opinions as to how things should be done. When differences lead to open conflicts—especially if they erupt while touring, just before a performance, or in the recording studio—the band has a huge problem. The manager is the ultimate problem solver when disputes arise among band members. As mediator, the manager at times has to struggle just to hold the band together.

Ensuring Security

Protecting musical instruments and equipment from theft and damage requires constant vigilance. The manager must see to it that band property is protected, both in public and in storage. Ultimately, the band will need to buy property and liability

MANAGEMENT QUESTIONS FOR EVERY BAND TO ASK

As popularity and momentum build, questions arise for every garage band. Here are some examples:

- Should the band members designate one among them to serve as manager, engage a nonperformer, or all pitch in with the non-musical tasks?
- How will the manager be paid?
- Who will make decisions concerning stage clothes, set lists, transportation arrangements, the placing of stage equipment, etc.? A manager, the band's recognized "natural leader," or all the members democratically?
- Who will handle the money, and how will it be divided?
- Onstage, who will function as leader or "front" musician—joking with the audience, introducing new songs, announcing upcoming performances or recording projects? (Someone needs to ram-rod the show, keeping things moving. You can lose an otherwise receptive audience if you allow too much dead time and bother-some tuning between songs.)

insurance; this likewise falls under the manager's long list of duties.

Cheerleading

Finally, the manager is the band's most devoted fan. The manager is a constant encourager and helper in small details. Disappointments are inevitable—unenthusiastic crowds, booking mistakes that put you in front of the wrong audiences, and so forth. When the players are feeling down, the manager has to pump them back up.

A band manager has to be a hard-nosed supervisor. At the same time, the manager must know how to encourage members of the band and road crew (and cut them some slack, if possible, when they're stressed). The manager must have a cheerful relationship with each member of the team.

Over time, successful bands accumulate a diverse management staff who have special individual skills. Most garage bands start out with one do-it-all manager. As they move into the semiprofessional and, eventually, professional arenas, they may acquire a management team of a half dozen or more specialists, from road manager to booking agent to lawyer.

Different Approaches to Management

Many start-up bands designate one or two of the players to manage all their operations. In some garage bands, everyone participates in one management function or another. Each member is on the lookout for bookings and promotional opportunities. They all pitch in to wrangle equipment. They share transportation. Certain members assume responsibility for specific duties (maintaining a Web site, designing flyers, writing press announcements, repairing equipment, etc.), depending on their skills and interests.

Almost all young bands have, if not a manager, a recognized leader. This person (or partnership, in some cases) sees to financial, legal, and general decision-making issues. The time will come, though, when the band will need someone who isn't immersed in the music to take care of the business.

The business process should begin with planning. Billy Mitchell, author of *The Gigging Musician*, says after a band becomes a functioning, rehearsed, marketable unit, "the next and most logical step should be sitting down to talk about issues, desires, and possibilities. This rarely happens. Musicians are into the music and want to leave legal issues to lawyers. We tend to expect things to work themselves out. But they don't."

Whatever goals you set, whatever plan you adopt, your band will need some form of management before it effectively can break free of the garage. Once the band decides how it will operate—who is responsible for what—a good manager can oversee it all and make sure everything goes according to plan.

ROAD WORK

Lots of garage bands wrangle their sound and stage equipment themselves when they play gigs. In some bands, one or two members volunteer for that duty; in others, all the musicians are expected to lend a hand. Eventually, as the band becomes successful, a road crew—or at least one hardy roadie—will be practical.

In some situations, the manager of a start-up band handles virtually all the group's nonmusical work, even slinging equipment. If a road crew is needed, it's the manager's responsibility to find reliable helpers.

Money will be an issue. Bill Henderson, author of *Running Your Rock Band*, discourages semi-professional bands from hiring a roadie. "The roadie is another mouth to feed, taking another slice of the money pie; as long as you can carry your own equipment around, pack it easily into somebody's van, and set it up without having a nervous breakdown, you should take advantage of the simplicity of this arrangement."

Equipment handlers aren't the only people a successfully performing and touring band will need, sooner or later. Here are examples of what's involved when you perform in public. All of them come under the general supervision of a manager.

Getting to Your Gig

Transportation is essential for a performing band. Each player must arrive at the gig venue early enough to relax, tune, make a sound check, and warm up. The equipment must be in place even earlier.

Garage bands typically travel together, with their equipment in tow. That means they have to arrive at the scene hours before they're scheduled to begin playing.

How do they travel? Many bands are able to invest in a used van or SUV to transport the musicians and support crew, with an enclosed trailer in which to haul equipment. Until they can afford to buy transportation of their own, they must borrow or rent it.

When the band goes full-time and begins to tour, transportation arrangements are more complicated. Will the band buy or rent a tour bus that has enough space to carry all of the equipment and provide compact living quarters?

ARRANGING TRANSPORTATION IS ONE OF MANY MANAGEMENT RESPONSI-
BILITIES. ROAD TIME SHOULD BE RELAXING FOR THE MUSICIANS AND
CREW; IT ALSO PROVIDES OPPORTUNITIES TO IMPROVE ARRANGEMENTS
AND TWEAK THE STAGE PRESENTATION.

Or will they use the van-and-trailer rig and include motel and
dining expenses in their operating budget?

An all-too-frequent crisis among bands is arriving at a
gig and learning, while setting up, that they've forgotten to
bring an essential item of equipment. To prevent this, make
a checklist of literally everything you'll need for the show.
This includes not just your instruments and heavy equipment,

but—especially—the small stuff: amp fuses, batteries, spare cables, carpet for the drum kit, guitar stands, music stands, paperwork (set lists, chorded music sheets, arrangement notes), and so on.

Print copies of the checklist and use it for every gig. The manager or roadie should check off each item as it's packed and double-check the list before leaving the garage.

Setting the Stage

Ideally, setting up for a performance should become a matter of routine. The manager or roadie (or stage manager, if the band has a separate helper for this task) determines each band member's personal space onstage, where the main and monitor speakers and any lighting equipment will be positioned, and where the control board will be. When the equipment is in place, cables are connected and secured, the sound system is tested, and the stage is ready for the band.

But complications almost always arise. No two stages are identical, and some are poorly designed. Author Bill Henderson comments, "Most stages are awkwardly shaped, too small for the average band, and disadvantageously placed for acoustics. Setting up is sometimes a multilevel engineering problem, so give yourself time to work it out— don't show up at the last minute." If you're performing at a nightclub or restaurant that's closed during the day, arrange with the owner or manager to let your road crew come in before hours.

ROAD CREWS PERFORM MANY TASKS BESIDES TOTING AND SETTING UP THE BAND'S EQUIPMENT. HERE, A CREW MEMBER CHANGES STRINGS FOR THE GUITARIST BACKSTAGE.

Solo and small ensembles occasionally find gigs where sound equipment is available for them onsite. It belongs either to the club or the organization for whom they're performing, or to a regular act whose members prefer to leave the equipment there and let guest musicians use it. Until you can afford to buy or rent your own system, your band may be restricted to performing in such stage-ready situations. It means a lot less work for you. On the other hand, apart from severely limiting your booking potential, it reduces your freedom to set up exactly the way you want.

Who Will Control Your Sound?

Auditoriums, nightclubs, civic halls, school gyms, malls, parking lots, backyards, and other places where garage bands perform sound differently. That means the settings of your sound system have to be adjusted from gig to gig. If you land a regular club gig, you may be able to find, in time, basic control settings that are satisfactory throughout your performance. The electric guitarist, bassist, and keyboardist can make individual adjustments in volume and effects from song to song. But if you use those same basic settings in a different room or outdoors, you'll probably find that the total output sounds different— possibly awful.

Lots of conditions affect how sound is distributed and absorbed in a given space, from the physical dimensions to the number of people in attendance. There's also the crowd noise factor.

If you could perform only in concert situations before fully attentive listeners, controlling your sound would be a lot easier. More often, garage bands find themselves playing in front of raucous audiences. Everyone is competing to be heard. The more people talking and laughing at once, the louder the crowd noise will be. The louder the crowd

AT A PACKED, NOISY PERFORMANCE VENUE, THE SOUND TECHNICIAN NEEDS TO BE OUT FRONT, HEARING EXACTLY WHAT THE AUDIENCE HEARS BUT IN A CONTROLLED SPACE, FREE OF INTERFERENCE.

noise becomes, the louder the band ramps up the master volume. As the music volume increases, people talk still louder, to the point of shouting. A few minutes into the first set, it's a screaming zoo.

Many solo, duo, and trio acts confine their performances to small rooms—bars, restaurants, and church and community gathering halls, where audiences typically number fewer than a hundred people and are relatively quiet, if not altogether attentive. They use basic sound systems consisting of a few microphones, a low-end control board, lightweight column

QUALITIES TO LOOK FOR IN A ROADIE

Your band may be so good and growing so fast in popularity that dozens of your friends and fans willingly would serve as regular roadies—perhaps for no pay. Beware! To a great extent, the work of a roadie is simply loading and unloading the band's equipment, placing it onstage, and packing it at the end of the show. Almost anyone with sufficient muscles can do most of this grunt work. It's advisable, though, to look for a roadie with experience and a lot more qualifications.

You want a roadie who does not aspire to join the band. You might be surprised at the number of starry-eyed fans who've learned a few guitar chords and feel that by volunteering, they should earn at least an audition.

In preparing for a performance, your roadie must keep an eye on the clock. The worker should allow more than enough time to transport your equipment and prepare your stage, leaving you at least half an hour before showtime for sound checks and tuning.

During the gig, the roadie should be focused constantly on the band, alert to needs and problems that might occur—not goofing around and socializing with fans and waitstaff. The ideal roadie is willing to serve as the musicians' gofer, supplying them with cold drinks while sweating under hot lights, scrambling to replace lost guitar picks and broken strings.

After the performance, the roadie should be able to pack the gear carefully but swiftly.

Personality-wise, the roadie should be a self-starter who's devoted to the work. The roadie should be courteous to everyone. Organizational, mechanical, and electrical skills are definite advantages. Casual dress is fine; bad hygiene and addictions are no-nos.

You do not want a roadie who is often late, moves slowly, forgets the basic equipment setup, critiques the band's music, uses foul language around strangers, and wears dirty clothes.

speakers, and one or two small monitor speakers at their feet. Their needs are nicely uncomplicated, compared with those of a six-piece band playing much larger gigs. In a small group/small setting, it's easy for one member of the group to control the sound board, making only occasional adjustments during the course of a set.

Larger outfits need a dedicated sound controller. This person knows the band's repertoire intimately, backward and forward. The sound technician runs the system continually during performances, adjusting settings from song to song to bring out the best possible effects. The technician can immediately correct volume discrepancies, feedback, and other ugly technical problems as they arise.

For some garage bands, the manager or roadie puts on the additional hat of sound technician during the performance. Eventually, though, the band may need an additional team member: a savvy, experienced sound person who knows the boards, the equipment, and—equally important—your music.

A word of warning—you may have a friend who just loves to play with sound, turning knobs to see what happens, often turning the wrong knobs cluelessly and worsening rather than correcting sound problems. Don't invite a passionate experimenter to run sound for you (even if the person will work for free).

MINDING THE MONEY

When the band begins playing for money, everything about music gets more complicated. At first thought, money management seems very simple. A five-member band splits the proceeds in five equal shares. A solo gets it all. Right?

Maybe, for the first gig or two. Then sticky questions start to arise.

Before they play for pay, the band should discuss issues like those described below. David Cutler, author of *The Savvy Musician*, considers "money matters" to be one part of an overall business plan. "What are your financial goals, and how will they be accomplished? A detailed budget should be included."

CHAPTER THREE

Issues of Ownership

In some bands, one member owns practically all the equipment, other than the instruments. This person also may own, or have the use of, a van and trailer. Typically, this individual is a veteran of another band that dissolved; he or she either "inherited" the sound system by default or bought out the interests of former bandmates.

Other bands go together to buy the system they need. In some cases, they pool their money and buy everything at once. In a few (unwise) situations, each member buys—and thereby owns—a particular item or items.

You can see how property ownership might have a huge effect on the band's finances and future sense of togetherness. Up front, the members should agree, in writing, on the terms of inventory. Who owns what, and how will everyone be compensated for its use?

Questions to ask yourselves: If one individual owns the whole system, will that person receive a greater slice of the income? If the equipment is owned by the band as a whole and a member quits, will the other members willingly buy out the departing player's share, or does the exiting musician lose his/her investment? What about any new member—a musician who hasn't contributed a dime for any of the equipment?

What if the equipment is owned individually, and the departing member owns, let's say, all the mic stands?

And hey, what about the member who owns, or whose family owns, the rehearsal garage or basement? Should that person receive a larger percent of the income?

You get the idea.

Dividing the Earnings

Your first earnings will come from live performances. Eventually—hopefully—you'll receive additional money selling band products including CDs and T-shirts. Divvying up the pay is no simple matter. You need to take the band's expenses into account. You also need to think ahead.

Paying the Musicians

Paying the musicians is obviously the most important thing. Players initially may presume they all will receive equal shares. But should they?

Besides the musician who owns the sound equipment and the one who provides the garage space, does anyone else deserve an extra cut? What of the musician who writes the band's original songs?

Paying the Manager

Full-time bands generally employ professional managers. A top manager may represent only one highly successful band, or as many as a half dozen local or regional bands. Some professionals run management companies, hiring lower-level managers to represent developing bands.

Other managers are basically amateurs, like the garage musicians for whom they work. The manager may be a close friend and fan of the musicians, an individual who holds down a day job but is willing to help the band after

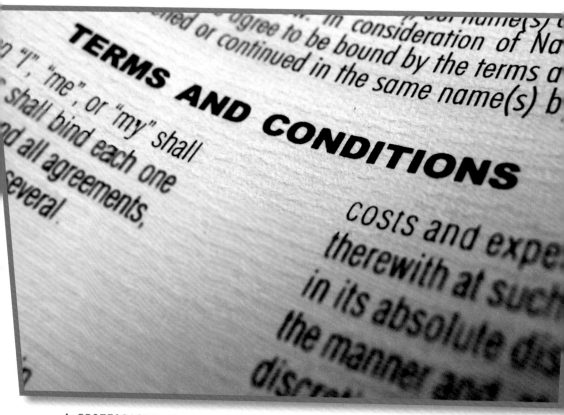

A PROFESSIONAL OR SEMIPROFESSIONAL BAND IS A BUSINESS. FORMAL, WRITTEN AND SIGNED AGREEMENTS CAN HELP EVEN START-UP GROUPS AVOID COSTLY CONFLICTS INVOLVING MUSICIANS, MANAGERS, EMPLOYERS, AND OTHERS.

hours. A friendly volunteer manager may suffice initially, but a thriving band soon will need a paid, dedicated manager.

In some bands, the manager receives an equal share of earnings with the musicians. In others, the manager receives a larger or smaller percentage.

Paying Other Team Members

Booking agents usually are paid on commission; they receive a percentage of what the gig pays. If the commission is 15 percent, the agent thus draws $75 for a $500 engage-ment. If your manager is also your agent, you need to determine whether this person will be paid separately for the two roles.

Most bands receive gig invitations through friends. This raises more money questions: If the band uses a book-ing agent, should the agent receive a commission for gigs that are obtained personally by a band member or friend? (Some agents think so.) Should the band refuse to negoti-ate any booking personally, turning every offer over to the agent immediately?

Don't underpay your roadie. Were it not for roadies, there wouldn't be many professional bands on tour. A good roadie who can also maintain your equipment and perform basic repairs can save you a lot of money.

Other team members who likely will be added to your payroll eventually include a lawyer and tax specialist.

Paying Expenses

You probably will incur business expenses before you first set foot onstage. Expenses include equipment purchases and repairs. Gas, meals, lodging, and auto maintenance will cost the band. There are promotional costs (for design-ing and printing business cards and flyers, etc.), Internet operating costs, and fees such as insurance.

When you're ready to record, your expenses will mount. Recording in a state-of-the-art studio is above the means of most fledgling garage bands. (To make your first basic

PROFESSIONAL RECORDING STUDIO TIME IS VERY EXPENSIVE. SKILLFUL TECHNICIANS IN HOME STUDIOS EQUIPPED WITH MODERN COMPUTER TECHNOLOGY CAN PRODUCE HIGH-QUALITY DEMO RECORDINGS AT MUCH LOWER COSTS.

demo CD, find a friend who has adequate recording equipment and computerized mixing software.)

Obviously, a portion of your income must be put aside for these expenses. As soon as you begin booking gigs, your band should establish a business bank account. Deposit all of your earnings into it and pay yourselves and your team members out of it. Leave an extra portion of each deposit in the account to cover expenses. You also should keep petty cash on hand for gas, meals, and other incidental expenses.

You may want to consider establishing two bank accounts: a checking account for payroll and routine expenses and a savings account for major future purchases.

Mind Your Tax Deductions

The federal government and most state governments tax citizens on the income they earn. Smart taxpayers keep receipts and careful records of their spending because the costs of many things they buy can be deducted (subtracted) from the total taxable income they must report to the government.

Certain home and office repair, home/office utility, health care, and educational expenses can be deducted. So can purchases that are necessary for you to do your work and earn money. For bands, legitimate business expenses may include the following:

- The costs of equipment, instruments, accessories, and repairs
- A small percentage of your rent or house payment, if an area of your home is used strictly for your music business (a rehearsal garage that's also used for auto storage probably will not be deductible)

31

- Travel expenses—gas, auto maintenance, meals, lodging
- Computer equipment and services you use exclusively for music-related business, including hardware and software purchases and repairs, Internet/e-mail access fees, the cost of hiring a professional Web designer, etc.
- Telephone service for band communications (if phone service is used for both personal and business calls, part of the costs may be deductible)
- Stereo equipment and music CDs you buy, if they're used for learning new songs and practicing your music
- Fees paid to photographers and graphic artists
- The costs of printing and mailing promotional materials
- Music lessons
- Clothes you wear onstage (if you wear them only onstage)

In short, anytime you spend money on behalf of the band, consider whether it might be a legitimate tax write-off.

Always obtain receipts. If a revenue service audits your tax returns, you'll be required to produce proof of your deducted purchases.

Some mathematics-loving, detail-oriented individuals prepare their own tax returns. Most musicians feel more

HOW QUICKLY WILL YOU BECOME RICH?

The more realistic question is: "Will you ever become rich?" The more successful the band becomes, the greater its expenses are and the more outside fingers there are reaching into the money pot.

Even if the band is offered a recording contract, the prospects for riches are iffy. Before you begin to earn significant royalties, the recording company has to recover its investment in you. Recording, promoting, and distributing a music project will cost somebody—the recording company or your band, if you choose to self-produce the album—a lot of money. In the book *Start Your Own Band*, author Marty Jourard points out the painful reality that "only a small percentage of CDs earn back their recording and production costs."

Although a recording is a wonderful thing to make available to fans, the real income for most bands is from live performances. Superstars earn big money through recordings and songwriting royalties. Lesser lights earn their incomes mainly on the road. It's fun for awhile, but in the long run, it's no easy way to make a living. For most musicians, it does not result in riches.

secure turning over their financial records to professional tax advisers or accountants. Besides keeping you straight with the government, a tax specialist can point out additional deductions you might have overlooked. A specialist can be particularly valuable in explaining which travel-related expenses are and aren't deductible.

Business Manager, Personal Manager— What's the Difference?

Who, exactly, will manage the band's checking or savings account and/or credit card?

Donald Passman defines a business manager as a person who "handles all your money." This individual receives all of the band's income, deposits it into the band's bank account, and pays each band member from the account. If the band needs new equipment, the business manager writes the check for it. The business manager also sorts out tax issues that affect the band as a unit.

Passman urges, "Be extremely careful in picking your business manager. More careful than you are with anyone else on your team."

A personal manager serves a different purpose. General decision making is the overriding duty. Specific activities range from concert preparation—seeing that everything is in place when the band takes the stage—and planning transportation to promoting the band to employers, agents, and recording companies. Passman notes, "A good personal manager can expand your career to its maximum potential, just as a bad one can rocket you into oblivion."

Most garage bands in their formative months and years don't employ both kinds of managers. They find one person who effectively can handle their business and banking transactions as well as personal matters.

LEGAL MATTERS

As you begin the business of performing, legal questions will arise. You won't need to retain a lawyer at first, but increasingly, you will need a legal professional who can guide you through contracts, payment disputes, and other issues.

Entertainment/media lawyers—those whose practices are based entirely on music, film, publishing, or other media affairs—are hard to find outside large cities. They are especially knowledgeable about 1) contract agreements and 2) intellectual property (creative works such as song lyrics and other writings, music compositions, band logos and T-shirt art, etc.). Because they know the ins and outs of the publishing and recording industries,

ORIGINAL MUSIC IS POTENTIALLY VALUABLE INTELLECTUAL PROPERTY. SONGWRITERS SHOULD COPYRIGHT THEIR WORKS. A LAWYER OR MANAGER EXPERIENCED IN THE MUSIC BUSINESS CAN HANDLE THESE AND OTHER LEGAL MATTERS FOR MUSICIANS.

they are especially important to songwriters and recording artists.

Many general practice (GP) lawyers won't take on musician clients because they aren't familiar with case law in that area. At the same time, most GPs can help you, to some extent. For example, they can review a contract for you and spot clauses that might cause problems for your band. They also may be able to help you choose the legal status of your band: partnership or corporation. (The way the band is legally organized affects its tax status, among other things. A lawyer can advise you on the details.)

The Band Members' Agreement

At first, few garage bands have any agreement. They just get together and play. As long as everyone basically behaves and cooperates, they can even launch their performing careers with no formal organization.

Soon, the first problems occur—tardiness, for instance. If a player is habitually late for rehearsals and gigs or wants to indulge in illegal substances during a show, it's time for everyone to sit down and establish ground rules, at least verbally.

Much larger issues are inevitable. If the band is serious about performing professionally, it's best to adopt a formal agreement, written and signed by everyone, early on. This can prevent stressful misunderstandings and even lawsuits.

Donald S. Passman, author of *All You Need to Know About the Music Business*, is a music industry lawyer. He describes the case of a well-known group who'd never adopted a formal agreement among the players. When one musician became unhappy and quit, he tried to prevent the band from using their established name. The court battle dragged on almost a decade, costing more than a million dollars in lawyer fees. "The group of course was killed early in the process, and the fellow who started the fight ended up broke. All of which could have been avoided with a simple agreement and a couple of hours of planning."

Issues to cover in the agreement should begin with basic responsibilities (like being on time). It should define income and expense sharing. It should explain the terms of property ownership, especially in regard to personnel changes. It should discuss how the band as a unit can go about hiring and firing. It should cover unforeseen crises. (What happens, for instance, if a member is unable to play for an extended period because of illness or injury? Will the band cancel bookings or find a substitute—or a permanent replacement?) It should address the rights of departing members. (Example: Should a former member who partici- pated in the recording of CDs receive a share of the profits from CD sales indefinitely?)

The Manager's Agreement

Band members should have complete trust in their man- ager, and the manager should be completely committed to the band. Although there should be no doubts between them, there should be a written agreement. When the band and manager part ways, a contract can avert the kinds of disputes that usually involve money.

The agreement should define the manager's duties and stipulate payment. If the manager is the band's main booking agent, the agreement should clarify whether the manager will receive added compensation for that.

Band-manager contracts may be reviewed and renewed annually. The agreement should discuss terms of ending

HIRING A LAWYER

When the time comes to engage a lawyer—and it will, if your band thrives—you should find one who understands how the music industry functions.

Entertainment lawyers usually charge by the hour for their services; $200 or more per hour is not unusual. Other lawyers charge bands a percentage of earnings (typically 5 percent). Some lawyers don't charge by the hour or expect a cut of the band's income, but work for a retainer fee. That is, the band pays them an agreed monthly fee to handle all legal matters.

Just because you have a professional entertainment lawyer, Donald Passman writes, don't expect the lawyer to find you shortcuts to fame. "If a record company doesn't like your music, they're not going to sign you because of your lawyer."

the relationship before the contract expires, in the event either party needs out.

Protecting Your Name

Before you begin your career, the band should research—or pay a lawyer to research—the name, to ensure it's original. (A Google search on the name is a good start but not conclusive.) After you're sure the name is clear, you'll want to protect it with a service mark. Simply using the name—having it associated with your band in the public mind—establishes your rights to it. Many groups take the further precaution of formally registering their names with the United States Patent & Trademark Office.

Decide what will happen to the band name when personnel change. For example, if half the members quit and organize a new group, can they take the name with them? If the founder of the band, who came up with the name, leaves, should that individual control the name?

Most bands operate by majority rule in such matters. Passman personally believes if one or more musicians are mainly responsible for establishing the band's sound, they should control the use of the name "because the others alone wouldn't truly represent the group to the public."

Protecting Your Music

Original music is a form of what lawyers call intellectual property. If members of the band are writing the group's material, they should protect this property by obtaining legal copyrights.

A copyright is literally the "right to copy" your music, which includes making copies of sheet music and recordings as well as presenting performances. The owner of a song's copyright owns all rights to perform, record, and otherwise copy the music. Anyone else who wishes to use the music must pay (or obtain the owner's permission).

The songwriter can obtain copyright information and registration material from the national Copyright Office, which is part of the Library of Congress (or online at www.

PERFORMANCE RIGHTS ORGANIZATIONS (PROS) COLLECT ROYALTIES FOR MUSICIANS AND SONGWRITERS. THEY ALSO HELP PROMOTE PERFORMERS THEY REPRESENT, STAGING EVENTS SUCH AS THIS SESAC SHOWCASE.

copyright.gov). Some songwriters prefer to handle this chore personally. Others delegate it to the band manager or lawyer.

Owning the song's copyright protects your creative property, but the copyright doesn't generate money for you. To be paid, you need to have it published. Legally, you deserve to be paid a tiny sum (pennies, literally), each time your song is performed in public—in nightclubs, concert halls, restaurants, or anywhere else. You also should be paid each time it is played on the radio or a recording of it is sold. These payments, called royalties, are miniscule, but they add up. The challenge is to collect the money, because you can't possibly trace every "copy" or instance of usage.

The way it's done is through a licensing, or performance rights, organization (PRO). These function something like musical collection agencies. Three companies serve this purpose in the United States: the American Society of Composers, Authors & Publishers (ASCAP); Broadcast Music, Inc. (BMI); and the Society of European Stage Authors and Composers (SESAC). (Despite its original "European" connotation, SESAC represents many major American songwriters and publishers.)

If you have your songs published by an established publishing company, the publisher typically takes care of your membership in the licensing organization with which it's affiliated. The licensing entity collects performance fees around the country and distributes shares of the income to writers and publishers.

Some songwriters and bands have formed their own small publishing companies.

Performing and Recording Contracts

Many hiring entities, notably large clubs and colleges, require bands to sign performance contracts. These deal not only with payment and the performance time and length, but with details that might not occur to you in advance. For example, will you be permitted to sell recordings, T-shirts,

DURING INTERMISSIONS AND BEFORE AND AFTER SHOWS, BANDS MAY BE ALLOWED TO SELL THEIR RECORDINGS, T-SHIRTS, MUGS, AND OTHER MERCHANDISE AND ADD NEW FANS TO THEIR PROMOTION LISTS.

and other band merchandise on the premises? If so, will you enjoy all the profit, or will the employer require a percentage? Will you be permitted to invite personal guests at no charge? How many?

Read the contract carefully. You probably can figure it out and decide for yourself whether it's acceptable. Such contracts, though, are another good reason to retain a lawyer.

Practically every aspiring musician harbors hopes of a recording career. Your first CD probably will be a demo. This is a basic recording of your best song, or several songs. Many bands make their first demos in the garage with low-cost, consumer-grade recording equipment. They burn copies to CDs and hand them to club owners, agents, the media, and anyone else who might further their careers.

The ultimate goal is to land a recording contract with an established label. Major recording companies regard up-and-coming bands as "baby bands." Occasionally, major labels pick up baby bands and give them a chance. Much more likely, a garage band's first recording success will be with a small indie label.

Whether the label is nationally prominent or regionally independent, no band should negotiate and sign a recording deal without a lawyer's advice.

Incidentally, just as you want to be paid for the use of your original material, other songwriters do, too. If you record someone else's song—even on a giveaway demonstration CD—you need to pay the PRO's usage fee.

Randy Chertkow and Jason Feehan, in their book *The Indie Band Survival Guide*, explain the requirements in detail. They note that special agencies are available to help bands locate publishers and pay the required fees, which can be done online.

SECURITY AND INSURANCE

A lot of things can go wrong in a music career. Besides handling personnel issues, technical problems, money shortages, and legal concerns, band management includes matters of security and insurance.

The band's manager often is expected to play a hands-on role in securing equipment. In addition, the manager acts as the band's representative in obtaining necessary insurance or finds an additional team member to advise the group on insurance needs.

Preventing Theft and Damage

The place where the band stores its equipment, whether it's the garage or a rented rehearsal room, may be a target of thieves.

Equipment can vanish overnight—or while the band members are taking a break during a gig. Musicians are personally responsible for the security of their musical instruments. Meanwhile, the group should have a policy for protecting its mutual property.

While the band is in performance, much of the responsibility for protecting the equipment falls on the roadie or road crew. The roadie should keep an eye on the stage when the band takes a break. Many a band's valuable essentials, including guitars and microphones, have walked during intermissions. While the band is performing, the roadie should watch the musicians' accessories—instrument cases, electronic tuners, backup gear—and personal items. Assume criminals are in attendance, watching for unguarded prizes.

Band members must be vigilant, too. The theft of musical instruments from parked, locked cars is an everyday occurrence. During breaks at performances, every musician, even while socializing with fans, should be mindful of the goods on and around the stage.

When a band is booked to perform on the same stage several consecutive nights, it's tempting to leave the equipment, including the drum set, at the scene overnight. The same is true if the band lands a permanent gig, playing one or more nights a week at a steady venue for an extended period. This saves hours of time, not to mention effort, in taking down and restaging the sound system and other effects. It's risky, though. Numerous bands have

FEW BANDS EXIST FOR LONG WITHOUT BAD EXPERIENCES, INCLUDING THEFT AND DAMAGED EQUIPMENT. INSURANCE POLICIES CAN EASE THE PAIN AND KEEP THE BAND IN BUSINESS WITHOUT INTERRUPTION.

horror stories of showing up to play a subsequent night of an extended gig and seeing the stage completely bare—and the manager of the facility pleads ignorance.

Bill Henderson, in *Running Your Rock Band*, suggests ways to minimize the danger while saving some of the repetitive legwork from night to night. "Take your mike, instruments, accessory pedals, and amplifier heads. The drummer should take the cymbals and perhaps the snare. Sometimes the club has a locked room for equipment, which reduces (although not totally) the possibility of theft. . . . And if you don't want your amps used on the sly by auditioning bands, take your fuses and fuse caps."

You should have a personal security policy during performances, especially if you play at dance clubs and parties. Careless dancers and people who get too rowdy might think it's exciting and attention-grabbing to stumble into your mic stands, amplifiers, and drum kit, but it could ruin your act. It also could cost you a lot of money. In serious incidents, you might recover some of your losses in a lawsuit for damages to your equipment. At the same time, the negligent dancer might sue you for personal injury, claiming your setup was unsafe.

Avoid the possibility with a "stay back" policy. If the audience becomes too rowdy, ask the manager to take control. If that fails, pull the plugs and pack your gear.

Types of Insurance

Bands buy different types of insurance, depending on their needs and where they are in their careers. Here are some of the forms of insurance you might consider.

Insuring Equipment

Each instrumentalist should insure the instrument against theft, loss, or damage. This may be as simple as adding a rider to your or your family's existing homeowner or renter property insurance policy. (The insurer may balk, however, if the theft occurs at a gig 100 miles [161 kilometers] from home.) Some companies specialize in small policies to insure musical instruments.

The band should insure its sound system and recording equipment. It also should maintain adequate insurance on its transportation: van, truck, SUV, and/or trailer.

If the band rents sound equipment or vehicles, it should buy renters' insurance to cover this property. (Note that a security deposit usually is required when renting vehicles.)

Andrew Thomas, a veteran musician and author of *Garage to Gigs: A Musician's Guide*, observes, "If you can afford insurance (and I don't think you can afford not to have it), you should get it. In addition to providing you with money to replace stolen or damaged equipment, it'll give you peace of mind the next time you leave your gear at your studio or in your car while you stop at a convenience store."

Thomas reports that he uses MusicPro Insurance, one company specializing in music-related policies, to insure his gear. His annual coverage costs 1 percent of what it would cost him to replace all of his equipment.

Insuring People

Most performance venues have personal injury and liability insurance. The band may want its own insurance, in case a musician is injured during a performance or in transit, or someone in the audience trips on your cabling and fractures a skull.

If music becomes your full-time, long-term career, you'll need other kinds of insurance. Health insurance is something young people rarely consider. They view it as something older people have. As for their own dental, visual, and infrequent emergency room needs, they're covered under their parents' policies. By the time you're in your mid-twenties, though, you'll have to buy your own health insurance (or work for an employer who buys it for you). Many professional bands obtain medical insurance at special group rates through music-related organizations such as the American Federation of Musicians.

Other Types of Insurance

Professional business managers usually have an "errors and omissions" (E&O) insurance policy covering their work. If the manager makes mistakes that cost the band money, this type of policy is intended to cover some or all of the losses.

Professional songwriters and publishers may want a special category of E&O insurance: insurance against claims that they've violated another writer's copyright. There are

ROCK GUITARIST JOE SATRIANI *(LEFT)* IN 2008 SUED THE BAND COLDPLAY *(RIGHT)*, CLAIMING THEIR HIT SONG "VIVA LA VIDA" SUBSTANTIALLY COPIED ELEMENTS OF A SONG HE WROTE SEVERAL YEARS EARLIER. SATRIANI AND COLDPLAY REACHED AN AGREEMENT BEFORE TRIAL.

only so many musical notes on the scale and so many ways to put them together into melodies. With millions of songs published, it's inevitable that some of the melodies (as well as phrases and whole lines of lyrics) are virtual duplicates.

SECURITY ONLINE

The band's presence on the Internet, because of the nature of the Net these days, can't be controlled entirely. Strangers as well as fans can grab photos, music clips, and personal details from your band's Web site or your page on Facebook or MySpace. They can disseminate your material all over the world—without your knowledge.

For the most part, this is a positive phenomenon, at least while you're in the process of making a name for your band. It amounts to free promotion. But the more successful you become, the more worrisome the wide-open Internet becomes.

At the least, you should see to it that your Web domain isn't violated. If your domain name is www.[yourbandname].com, make sure no one establishes a rogue domain at www.[yourbandname].net. Perform frequent searches on your band's name to learn where and how you're being talked about on the Internet. You may want to bar access to certain parts of your Web site, permitting only registered fans and others to access those areas with passwords.

Peter M. Thall, an entertainment lawyer and author of *What They'll Never Tell You About the Music Business*, states, "I do not know of a successful artist who has not faced a claim of copyright infringement." Insurance against copyright infringement, Thall says, is "fairly expensive, but definitely worth considering."

The Well-Managed Band

Even during the jamming-in-the-garage period, a start-up band can have more fun if it applies a little organization. If the bass player and drummer have to wait around half an hour for the other people to show up, they probably won't be in the best of moods. The band will make faster progress once individual members begin assuming responsibilities for arranging songs, planning rehearsals, making practice recordings, and other things. Having a leader with the accepted authority to tell the guitarist to turn it down and the bass player to get in tune definitely helps.

When musicians enter the demanding, competitive realm of professional performance, effective band management becomes essential. The band still needs its leader, arranger, and personnel policy. But now, it also needs a team of supporting nonmusicians. They will take care of the business side of music, from handling equipment and running the sound board to tracking tax deductions to obtaining copyrights to guarding the property.

In the garage, it's just the players. Out there, the players are part of a larger organization. The better it's managed, the greater the likelihood it will succeed.

A&R Artist and repertoire; A&R representatives scout for new talent for recording companies.

AGENT A person who represents a band or individual in finding gigs or recording deals.

CASE LAW Law that is established on the basis of previous verdicts.

COMMISSION A percentage of profits paid to an agent or representative.

CORPORATION A group legally authorized to act as one, with certain privileges and liabilities.

DEMO A promotional recording of a band's best song or songs, often homemade, to give to prospective employers, agents, recording companies, and media.

ENTITY An organization, such as a business or governmental unit, that has an identity that is separate from those of its members.

GENERAL PRACTITIONER A lawyer who represents clients in a variety of cases, focusing on no particular area of law.

GIG An entertainer's booked engagement.

INDIE Independent; in music, a band or performer who works without a major recording contract; also, a small, usually regional recording company.

INTELLECTUAL PROPERTY Property, such as writing and music, that is created in the mind rather than from physical sources.

LABEL The name (brand) of an established recording company.

MEDIATOR A person who steps in to resolve a dispute.

MONITOR A small speaker pointed toward the stage rather than toward the audience, helping musicians hear their sound as the audience hears it.

PARTNERSHIP Two or more people legally associated as principals in a business.

RAUCOUS Making or constituting a disturbingly harsh and loud noise.

REPERTOIRE All the songs a band can play.

RETAINER A fee paid in advance to engage a lawyer's services as needed.

ROADIE A person who transports and handles a band's equipment for performances.

ROYALTY A songwriter, publisher, or recording artist's share of music sales income.

SET A selection of songs from a band's repertoire.

SOUND CHECK A band's test of each instrument and microphone with the sound system before performing.

TAX DEDUCTION A portion of income that is not taxable.

VENUE The place where an event is held; for example, a performing arts center is a venue for a concert.

The American Society of Composers, Authors & Publishers
    (ASCAP)
One Lincoln Plaza
New York, NY 10023
(212) 621-6000
Web site: http://www.ascap.com
The primary music licensing and royalty distribution organi-
    zation, ASCAP provides information and resources for
    songwriters and publishers.

Broadcast Music, Inc. (BMI)
7 World Trade Center
250 Greenwich Street
New York, NY 10007-0030
(212) 220-3000
Web site: http://bmi.com
A licensing and distributing organization that is for song-
    writers and publishers.

National Arts Centre
P.O. Box 1534, Stn B
Ottawa, ON K1P 5W1
Canada

(613) 947-7000
(866) 850-2787
Web site: http://www.nac-cna.ca
This Canadian government institution is dedicated to all perform-
    ing arts.

Society of European Stage Authors and Composers (SESAC)
55 Music Square East
Nashville, TN 37203
(615) 320-0055
Web site: http://www.sesac.com
This is a licensing and distributing organization for songwriters and
    publishers.

United States Copyright Office
101 Independence Avenue SE
Washington, DC 20559-6000
(202) 707-3000
(877) 476-0778
Web site: http://www.copyright.gov
This is the federal agency that administers copyright law.

Web Sites

Due to the changing nature of Internet links, Rosen Publishing has
developed an online list of Web sites related to the subject of this
book. The site is updated regularly. Please use this link to access
the list:

http://www.rosenlinks.com/gaba/mgmt

Anderson, Marisa, ed. *Rock 'n Roll Camp for Girls: How to Start a Band, Write Songs, Record an Album, and Rock Out!* San Francisco, CA: Chronicle Books, 2008.

Anderson, Sheila E. *How to Grow as a Musician: What All Musicians Must Know to Succeed.* New York, NY: Allworth Press, 2005.

Anderson, Stephen, et al. *So You Wanna Be a Rock Star? How to Create Music, Get Gigs, and Maybe Even Make It BIG!* Hillsboro, OR: Beyond Words Publishing, 1999.

Bidini, Dave. *For Those About to Rock: A Road Map to Being in a Band.* Plattsburgh. New York: Tundra Books, 2004.

Black, Sharon. *The Gigs Handbook: A Beginner's Guide to Playing Professionally.* Evanston, IL: Benny Publishing, 2000.

Bliesener, Mark, and Steve Knopper. *The Complete Idiot's Guide to Starting a Band.* New York, NY: Alpha (Penguin Group), 2004.

Buttwinick, Marty. *Starting Your First Band* (The Musicians' How-To Series). Glendale, CA: Sonata Publishing, 2008.

Gerardi, Robert. *Opportunities in Music Careers.* Chicago, IL: VGM Career Books/McGraw-Hill, 2002.

Gervais, Rod. *Home Recording Studio: Build It Like the Pros.* 2nd ed. Boston, MA: Course Technology PTR, 2011.

Gipi. *Garage Band.* New York, NY: First Second Books (Holtzbrinck Publishers), 2007.

Hall, Barbara. *Tempo Change.* New York, NY: Delacorte Press, 2009.

Hopper, Jessica. *The Girls' Guide to Rocking: How to Start a Band, Book Gigs, and Get Rolling to Rock Stardom.* New York, NY: Workman Publishing Company, 2009.

Johnson, Arne, and Karen Macklin. *Indie Girl: From Starting a Band to Launching a Fashion Company.* San Francisco, CA: Zest Books (Orange Avenue Publishing), 2008.

Mitchell, Billy. *The Gigging Musician: How to Get, Play, and Keep the Gig.* San Francisco, CA: Backbeat Books, 2001.

Powell, Stephanie. *Hit Me With Music: How to Start, Manage, Record, and Perform With Your Own Rock Band.* Brookfield, CT: Millbrook Press, 1995.

Schwartz, Daylle Deanna. *Start and Run Your Own Record Label.* 3rd ed. New York, NY: Billboard Books, 2009.

GAIN TREBLE BODY DRIVE SELECT BASS VOLUME REVERB FOOT SWITCH VACUUM TUBE DISTORTION POWER ON MADE IN U.S.A.

"Band Manager: Job Description, Duties and Requirements."
    Education-Portal.com. Retrieved April 2011 (http://
    education-portal.com/articles/Band_Manager_Job_
    Description_Duties_and_Requirements.html).

Chertkow, Randy, and Jason Feehan. *The Indie Band Survival
    Guide: The Complete Manual for the Do-It-Yourself
    Musician.* New York, NY: St. Martin's Griffin, 2008.

Citron, Stephen. *Song Writing: A Complete Guide to the
    Craft, Revised & Updated.* New York, NY: Limelight
    Editions/Hal Leonard Corporation, 2008.

Cutler, David. *The Savvy Musician: Building a Career,
    Earning a Living, & Making a Difference.* Pittsburgh,
    PA: Helius Press, 2010.

Henderson, Bill. *Running Your Rock Band: Rehearsing,
    Financing, Touring, Succeeding.* New York, NY:
    Schirmer Books/Simon & Schuster MacMillan, 1996.

Jourard, Marty. *Start Your Own Band: Everything You
    Need to Know to Take Your Band to the Top.* New
    York, NY: Hyperion, 1997.

"Multi-Platinum Musician Mark Bryan Teaches at the
    College." Press release, College of Charleston,
    Office of Media Relations, October 9, 2009.

"Music Manager and Management Rolls." Artist
    Management Resource. Retrieved April 2011

(http://www.artistmanagementresource.com/music-manager-roles.html).

Passman, Donald S. *All You Need to Know About the Music Business, Revised & Updated*. New York, NY: Free Press (Simon & Schuster Inc.), 2006.

Rwakaara, Jeremy. "8 Reasons Why a Band or Artist Needs a Manager." Artist Management Resource. Retrieved April 2011 (http://www.artistmanagementresource.com/helpful-articles/29-8-reasons-why-a-band-or-artist-needs-a-manager.html).

Thall, Peter M. *What They'll Never Tell You About the Music Business: The Myths, the Secrets, the Lies (& a Few Truths)*. New York, NY: Billboard Books/Watson-Guptill Publications, 2006.

Thomas, Andrew. *Garage to Gigs: A Musician's Guide*. New York, NY: Billboard Books/Watson-Guptill Publications, 2008.

Unterberger, Richie. "Garage Rock." Allmusic.com. Retrieved February 2011 (http://www.allmusic.com/explore/essay/garage-rock-t539).

Waterman, Chris. "Rock Music." Microsoft Student 2008 [DVD]. Redmond, WA: Microsoft Corporation, 2007.

Weissman, Dick. *Making a Living in Your Local Music Market: Realizing Your Marketing Potential*. Milwaukee, WI: Hal Leonard Corporation, 1999.

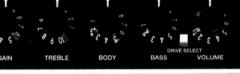

INDEX

A

American Federation of
   Musicians, 50
American Society of Composers,
   Authors & Publishers
   (ASCAP), 42
Anderson, Sheila E., 10

B

band managers
   requirements of, 6, 10, 14
   responsibilities of, 8–14, 16,
      41, 45
booking agents, 8, 10, 14,
   28–29, 38
Broadcast Music, Inc. (BMI), 42
business managers, 7, 34

C

checklist of equipment, creating,
   18–19
Chertkow, Randy, 44
contracts/agreements
   band members' agreement,
      37–38
   manager's agreement, 38–39
   performing and recording
      contracts, 12, 33, 42–44

copyright/music protection,
   40–42, 50–52, 53
Cutler, David, 25

D

disputes, resolving, 12–13

E

earnings, how to divide, 27–31

F

Feehan, Jason, 44

H

Henderson, Bill, 16, 19, 48

I

insurance, 13–14, 48–52

J

Jourard, Marty, 5, 10, 33

L

lawyers, 7–8, 12, 14, 15, 29,
   35–37, 39, 41, 43, 44

licensing/performing rights organization (PRO), 42, 44

M

management
  different approaches to, 14–15
  questions to ask about, 13
Mitchell, Billy, 15
MusicPro Insurance, 49

N

name of band, researching and trade-marking, 39–40
negotiation, 12, 29, 44

O

ownership of equipment, 25–26

P

Passman, Donald, 7, 34, 37, 39, 40
personal managers, 7, 34
promotion, 8, 10–12, 15, 33, 52
publicity, 8–9, 10

R

roadies, 7, 8, 16, 19, 24, 29, 46
  qualities to look for in, 23

S

security, 13–14, 45–48, 53
Society of European Stage Authors and Composers (SESAC), 42
sound systems, 16, 19, 20–21, 21–24, 26, 49
stage setup, 8, 10, 16, 19–21, 26

T

taxes/tax deductions, 31–33, 53
Thall, Peter M., 52
Thomas, Andrew, 49
transportation to and from gigs, 9, 15, 17–19

W

Web sites/domain names, 15, 52

About the Author

Daniel E. Harmon has performed solo and in groups of different genres at festivals, college concerts, nightclubs, school programs, and in other settings. He has composed and recorded soundtracks for public television projects and recorded several albums. A widely published music reviewer and founder of the *Hornpipe* folk music magazine, he has taught several instruments privately and in classes. Harmon is the author of more than seventy books.

Photo Credits

Cover (band), cover and interior background image (club), pp. 11, 28, 36 Shutterstock.com; p. 5 Marissa Kaiser/Stone/Getty Images; p. 9 Digital Vision/Thinkstock; p. 18 Fuse/Getty Images; p. 20 Andrew Lepley/Redferns/Getty Images; p. 22 Michael Tullberg/Getty Images; p. 30 Naki/Redferns/Getty Images; p. 41 Jerritt Clark/WireImage/Getty Images; p. 43 © Sean Haffey/San Diego Union Tribune/ZUMA Press; p. 47 Creatas/Thinkstock; p. 51 (left) Christie Goodwin/Getty Images; p. 51 (right) Nick Pickles/WireImage/Getty Images; back cover and interior graphic elements: © www.istockphoto.com/Adam Gryko (radio dial), © www.istockphoto.com/Tomasz Zajaczkowski (amp), © www.istockphoto.com/sammyc (drum set silhouette), Shutterstock.com (cable, frequency bar), © www.istockphoto.com/spxChrome (stage pass), © www.istockphoto.com/Bryan Faust (foot pedal).

Designer: Nicole Russo; Editor: Kathy Kuhtz Campbell;
Photo Researcher: Karen Huang